Forgiveness

BY CYNTHIA AMOROSO

The Child's World

Published by The Child's World®
1980 Lookout Drive • Mankato, MN 56003-1705
800-599-READ • www.childsworld.com

Acknowledgments
The Child's World®: Mary Berendes, Publishing Director
The Design Lab: Design
Pamela J. Mitsakos: Photo Research
Christine Florie: Editing

Photographs ©: David M. Budd Photography: 5, 9, 15, 17, 21;
iStockphoto.com/Barracuda Designs:19; iStockphoto.com/francisblack:
11; iStockphoto.com/Kali Nine LLC: 7; iStockphoto.com/Nicole S. Young:
cover, 1; iStockphoto.com/steex: 13.

ISBN 9781623235178
LCCN 2013931772

Printed in the United States of America
Mankato, MN
July, 2013
PA02172

ABOUT THE AUTHOR

Cynthia Amoroso is Director of Curriculum and Instruction for a school district in Minnesota. She enjoys reading, writing, gardening, traveling, and spending time with friends and family.

Table of Contents

What Is Forgiveness?   4

Forgiveness at School   6

The Teasers   8

Feeling Disappointed   10

Mistakes Happen   12

Letting Go of Bad Feelings   14

Brothers and Sisters
   Need Forgiveness, Too   16

Forgiving Yourself   18

Forgiveness Is Not Always Easy!   20

Glossary   22

Learn More   23

Index   24

What Is Forgiveness?

Sometimes people do things that make you feel angry. Sometimes they say or do things that hurt your feelings. Forgiveness means letting go of hurt feelings. When you forgive people, you stop being angry at them. You **accept** their mistakes.

Being able to forgive someone means to let go of hurt feelings.

Forgiveness at School

Imagine that you just got a new book. You cannot wait to read it! You bring it to school to read during library time. Your friend borrows the book. But she forgets to give it back. When she remembers, she says she is sorry. You show forgiveness by not staying mad. You show forgiveness by saying, "That's OK."

We can show forgiveness by not staying angry.

The Teasers

Have you ever been **teased**? Teasing can make people mad. It can hurt their feelings. Imagine that some kids are teasing you. They are making fun of something you did or said. One of your friends starts teasing you, too. Later she says she is sorry. You show forgiveness by not staying angry at her.

Sometimes people forget that teasing can hurt.

Feeling Disappointed

You feel good when your parents come to your hockey games. You want them to see you win. But what if your team loses? Maybe other kids on the team made lots of mistakes. You feel **disappointed** that you lost. You might feel angry at the other kids. But you show forgiveness by not getting upset. You understand that nobody wins every time.

Everybody loses sometimes. Maybe your team will win next time!

Mistakes Happen

Your teacher is getting her classroom ready for a school party. Some kids cause trouble by playing with the food. Your teacher thinks you were one of them. She is angry and scolds you. You feel hurt. You know you did not do anything wrong. Soon your teacher finds out what really happened. You show forgiveness by not being angry at her. You understand that even teachers can make mistakes.

Letting Go of Bad Feelings

You draw a beautiful chalk picture on the sidewalk. You want to show your mom. You go inside to get her. Your neighbor is watering her yard. She washes off the picture with her hose. You are angry and sad. But you understand that the neighbor made a mistake. She did not know you wanted to keep the picture. You show forgiveness by letting go of your anger and sadness.

Most people do not hurt our feelings on purpose.

Brothers and Sisters Need Forgiveness, Too

Maybe your brother likes to pick on you. He grabs your **favorite** toy and takes it outside. But he forgets to bring it back in! That night, it rains. Your toy gets wet and muddy. Your brother feels bad. He did not mean to ruin the toy. He tells you he is sorry. You forgive him.

Sometimes forgiving people can be hard.

Forgiving Yourself

You are visiting your grandpa's house. You reach for a cookie and knock a vase off the table. You feel really bad! You would never do something like that on purpose. But this was an **accident**. You tell your grandpa you are sorry. He understands that it was an accident. He forgives you. And you forgive yourself. You will be more careful next time!

Accidents can help us learn to be more careful.

Forgiveness Is Not Always Easy!

It can be hard to forgive people. You might feel angry or sad or disappointed. Sometimes it is hard to let go of those feelings. But when you do, you feel better. You help the other person feel better, too. Forgiveness helps people get along.

Forgiveness helps people get rid of bad feelings.

Glossary

accept–When you accept something, you understand that it cannot be changed.

accident–An accident is something that happens–but not on purpose..

disappointed–Feeling disappointed is feeling unhappy that something you wished for did not happen.

favorite– When you like something best, it is your favorite.

teased–When you are teased, someone makes fun of you.

Learn More

Books

Berenstain, Jan. *The Berenstain Bears and the Forgiving Tree*. Grand Rapids, MI: Zonderkidz, 2011.

Taylor, Jeannie. *Am I Forgiving?* Grand Rapids, MI: Kregel Kidzone, 2007.

Thompson, Lauren. *The Forgiveness Garden*. New York: Feiwel and Friends, 2012.

Web Sites

Visit our Web site for links about forgiveness: childsworld.com/links

Note to Parents, Teachers, and Librarians: We routinely verify our Web links to make sure they are safe and active sites. So encourage your readers to check them out!

Index

Accepting mistakes, 4, 12, 14
accidents, 18

Being more careful, 18

Family, 16, 18
feeling angry, 4, 8, 10, 12, 14, 20
feeling disappointed, 10, 20
feeling hurt, 4, 8, 12
feeling sad, 14, 20
friends, 6, 8

Hockey, 10

Neighbor, 14

School, 6, 12

Teacher, 12
teasing, 8